SOUL DEVELOPMENT THROUGH HANDWRITING

Soul Development Through Handwriting

The Waldorf Approach to the Vimala Alphabet

Jennifer Crebbin

STEINERBOOKS

2007

SteinerBooks
AN IMPRINT OF ANTHROPOSOPHIC PRESS, INC.
610 MAIN STREET, SUITE 1
GREAT BARRINGTON, MA 01230
www.steinerbooks.org

Copyright © 2007 by Jennifer Crebbin. All rights reserved.
Except where indicated, no part of this publication may be reproduced, stored in a retrieval
system, or transmitted in any form or by any means, electronic, mechanical,
photocopying, recording, or otherwise without prior
written permission of the publisher.

COVER AND BOOK DESIGN BY WILLIAM (JENS) JENSEN
COVER IMAGE BY LEAH GROISBERG :: AUTHOR PHOTO BY THOMAS BACKER

LIBRARY OF CONGRESS CATALOGING-IN-PUBLICATION DATA
Crebbin, Jennifer.
  Soul development through handwriting : the Waldorf approach to the Vimala alphabet / Jennifer Crebbin.
     p. cm.
  Includes bibliographical references (pp. 110–111).
  ISBN-13: 978-0-88010-587-3
  ISBN-10: 0-88010-587-9
  1. Graphology. 2. Waldorf method of education. 3. Children—Writing. 4. Rodgers, Vimala. I. Title.
  BF901.C74 2007
  155.2'82—dc22

                                                         2007034190

Table of Contents

Acknowledgements

First and foremost, I want to thank Dr. Vimala Rodgers, who during the first class I took from her said, "I need someone from the Waldorf Community to introduce my work to them." Without Vimala Rodgers' pioneering work in this field, I would not have changed my life by changing my own handwriting, and certainly would not have written this book. I live in admiration of her vision, intelligence, and fortitude. I thank you with all my heart for all you have given me!

My sincere appreciation to Rudolf Steiner for the wisdom he has shared with the world, as the founder of so many new branches of learning, but especially for his work in education and biodynamic agriculture.

Thanks to my husband Daniel for his patience and understanding when I quit my job to write, and to my dear friend Lisa Schrader for her interest in my process and her skillful writing support.

To all those who helped me collect information, especially Judith Soleil, librarian at the Rudolf Steiner Library. To all my friends and supporters who believed in me from the beginning. My sincere thanks goes to all those who read my manuscript and gave me valuable feedback: Paula Moraine, Dominique Vorlet, Vimala Rodgers, Penni Sparks, Lynne Poirier, Declan Owens, and Ingun Schneider.

And, thanks to you, the reader, for opening this book to see what it contains.

Rudolf Steiner on Education and Handwriting

"In regard to handwriting, it is so that people do not have a writing, rather the writing has the person... That means, we have in our wrist, in our hand, a certain writing trait. We write mechanically out of our hand. This fetters the human being. The human being becomes unfettered when he writes in the way that he paints or draws, when each letter next to the other becomes something that he draws."

ROSICRUCIANISM AND MODERN INITIATION

"The reverence that is needed to make education effective, something that can take on a religious quality, will arise if you as a teacher are conscious that when around the seventh year you call forth from the child's soul the forces that are used when the child learns to draw and to write, these actually come down from heaven!"

BALANCE IN TEACHING

"Our rightful place as educators is to be removers of hindrances."

THE SPIRITUAL GROUND OF EDUCATION, LECTURE IV

"Each child in every age brings something new into the world from the divine regions, and it is our task as educators to remove bodily and physical obstacles out of its way: to remove hindrances so that his spirit may enter in full freedom into life."

THE SPIRITUAL GROUND OF EDUCATION, LECTURE IV

"We must work on our etheric bodies. We must transform the qualities of our temperament to the extent that we can, for instance, consciously alter our movements, our gait and our handwriting. It is not enough to become a more ethical person. We must become a different person."

ISIS MARY SOPHIA: HER MISSION AND OURS

"Take for example, writing. The boy writes something like this, does he not? Now it will be for you to set to work and take the utmost care and pains that he shall gradually change his handwriting and develop it into a finely formed script. And you will find that while he is doing this, there will be clear signs also of a transformation taking place in his whole inner constitution."

CURATIVE EDUCATION, LECTURE XI

The Vimala Alphabet

A a   B b   C c   D d   E e ε

F f   G g   H h   I i   J j   K k

L l   M M m   N N n   O o

P p   Q q   R r   S s   T T   U u

V v   W W w   X x   Y y   Z z

Introduction

The times ahead will place demands on our children as never before. Life forces will be required to see clearly the choices available to them, evaluating their consequences and implications. They will be asked to sort through and prioritize vast quantities of information to deal with a rapidly changing world. With the steady stream of impressions from television, computers, movies, Xboxes, iPods, and so on, the young child is constantly bombarded with nerve-sense impressions that can have a lasting, deadening effect on young bodies. Children fortunate enough to have parents who provide a safe haven from continual sensory input are becoming increasingly rare in this country today.

Children who are taught by the Waldorf method, whether at home, in the public system, or in an AWSNA school (Association of Waldorf Schools in North America), are fortunate to be in an educational system that has many not just nourishing but truly healing aspects in its curriculum and educational methods. Waldorf education contains a profound capacity to provide the kind of stimulation most suitable for growing children through a curriculum based on real insights into child development, with a deep concern for the long-range goals of education: to foster development toward becoming free-thinking, actively engaged, and warm-hearted adults. The aim of Waldorf education is to ensure that students develop all of their potential.

Over the last twenty-one years, I provided Waldorf education for my three children, following their education as a parent and, at times, as an administrator or the wife of a specialty teacher. When I discovered the Vimala Alphabet, I saw the power of the marriage with Waldorf education. After earning my certification as a Handwriting Consultant, teaching classes, and working one-on-one with handwriting clients, I developed a passion for introducing this work to the Waldorf school movement. Open hearts have met me all along my path.

Audrey McAllen's excellent book *Teaching Children Handwriting* has long been *the* book on how to approach the subject of handwriting in the classroom, but does not go into detail about which style of writing to teach, except that it should be upright and rounded. This is a critical question, because when we write we not only express through the forms of the letters how we see ourselves and the world, but we also reinforce it. Many teachers choose the Palmer or revised Palmer style, which was first developed in 1895 and reflects all the values of that materialistic time. The Palmer Alphabet was created when the world was a radically different place. It can reinforce the qualities of greed, fear, and jealousy, to mention a few, every time it is used for writing. Children of the twenty-first century deserve something different. The D'Nealian Alphabet is also a popular choice, but still includes many of the repressive qualities of the Palmer Alphabet.

I bring a new choice to the Waldorf community. The Vimala Alphabet was first made public in 1995 by Dr. Vimala Rodgers, an Alphabetician and educator. She shares with us forms of the letters that support us in expressing our finest human qualities. Dr. Rodgers' goal is to create a world so harmonious that intolerant behavior would be shocking. When we teach the Vimala Alphabet to children, we help them preserve their connection to their innate spiritual wisdom and express their noblest human traits. It helps remove hindrances to the full expression of one's unique Self by supporting soul development. On the pages that follow, I offer the basic tools for teaching children a form of handwriting that will support the development of healthy human qualities: tolerance, service to others, compassion, direct communication, trust, and creative expression. My vision is that, through this work, we can create a world of individuals living in peaceful community.

This way of writing has a profound impact, whether taught to children learning to write or to adults later in life. When adults change their handwriting, they uncover hidden talents and gifts with amazing speed. The process is miraculous—but that is a different book.

This book has five parts. Part one summarizes the available literature on introducing handwriting to your class plus a few insights of my own. Part two covers the vocabulary, or "terms of art," the terms needed to understand the rest of the book. Part three covers each letter, with a description of the qualities or meaning of each letter, including examples of when a student may need to focus on a certain letter and how to form each letter. This section gives guidelines for identifying and removing hindrances in the children under Supporting Soul Development. Part four gives examples of undesirable forms and the corrections needed. Part five contains pages that may be copied and distributed in the classroom as practice pages. Although these pages are copyrighted, along with the rest of the book, you have my permission to copy these practice pages for use in your class. Please do not copy other pages in this book. In the appendix, I have included a form to assist in looking at students' handwriting and evaluating the changes needed. It has been developed for inclusion in the teachers' year end reports to the parents.

The Vimala Alphabet is already being used in many Waldorf settings in North America. One teacher, Carole Street, pioneered this work at Brightwater School in Seattle, Washington. Her premature death in 2006 prevented her from realizing her dream of carrying this work forward to the Waldorf community. In her own words:

> In my teaching I incorporate much that I and my colleagues feel will strengthen the character and capacities of the children. I know that Vimala's cursive has added an extra dimension in this quest. When the Vimala Alphabet was introduced to me, I immediately had a deep appreciation for its beauty and the premise upon which it is based. I taught it to my current class four years ago as their first cursive alphabet, and have continued with it to the present. My Grade 6 class is in great shape. In fact, this class is widely acknowledged as a leading light in our North Western U.S. Waldorf school community. On top of that, they are the most loving and compassionate class, and the best-behaved class in our school. Who knows how much how they write has added to their development, but added it has!

This writing technique supports and strengthens everything Waldorf education works toward. The Vimala Alphabet supports the child in becoming a conscious human being by supporting the soul's development. This simple shift in writing styles can transform, awaken, and develop the capacities children need in order to thrive. I invite you to take this sacred technology into your classroom and witness for yourself the amazing results.

Please join me on this journey.

Part One: Teaching the Letters

Form Drawing: The Straight Line and the Curve

I remember my youngest daughter coming home from school and telling me she had learned all the letters in school that day. Knowing how slowly the letters are introduced in the curriculum, this surprised me, and I said, "Oh really? Show me." She proceeded to draw a straight line and a curve. In her mind, she had learned all the letters!

Waldorf teachers begin teaching the letters by exploring these two basic shapes, the straight line and the curve. The goal is to integrate these two forms as deeply as possible before introducing the specific letters. They typically ask that the class walk these two forms and draw them with their feet; the children experience the straight line and the curve on the blackboard and on the floor.

Then, they explore where these forms live in their bodies. The curves are in their head and in the curved arms, while the straight lines live in the spine and straight limbs. The children lie on the floor in straight lines, then in curves, feeling these forms in their bodies.

We can divide space in six ways in our three-dimensional reality. Think of the sides of a box. The vertical line divides left from right, while the horizontal line divides space into above and below, and a slanted line divides space into front and back. It is important for young children to experience all these types of lines, which they can do in form drawing and writing. The movement from left to right strengthens the physical body; it is not only the direction in which we write, but is also included in the final stroke of many letters in the Vimala Alphabet.

Presenting the Letters

By introducing the letters with a gesture or picture, one by one, the children cultivate a reverence for each letter. Taking care and time in presenting letters in this way provides children with lifelong memories, as well as a reference point for the pronunciation of the letters, which is so useful in spelling. The consonants are presented as an image in the shape of the letter that begins with the sound of the letter, while a gesture or image introduces the vowels. Twenty years later, my oldest daughter can still recall the images first given her as she learned the letters.

Here I would like to introduce an idea that we will return to later. Imagine a cat curled up, drawn with the letter C to represent the curved spine. One could use cat as an image to represent the letter C, since this letter is shaped in a curve, like the spine of a curled-up cat, and carries one of the sounds of this letter. Now to expand on this, we can add an additional element, the quality of the letter, as explained in the following pages, drawing on both Steiner's indications and the Vimala Alphabet. Each letter has spiritual qualities. The letter C carries in our handwriting the quality or meaning of complete trust, particularly in regard to our relationships with the feminine world. In this way we can express not only the shape and image with the sound of the letter, but also express the quality contained in each letter.

For K, the image of a king could be used, as one who rules and, at the same time, recognizes his responsibility to those he governs. The letter K represents the right relationship to authority, not rebelling, being a tyrant, or buckling under. One can easily see for P a lovable Prince who fully and freely forgives everyone, with his upright stem and sweeping forward stroke? The letter P shows us self-lovability and acceptance. These are only a few examples to encourage your creativity in developing the images for the letters that contain the sound and shape of the letter, while carrying a sense of the quality of the letter.

Exercises

These exercises can be used with your class to begin teaching writing. They will assist the children in taking the forms into their bodies, whether the beginning shapes of the straight line and the curve or, later, the letters.

Students can draw the straight line and the curve in the air. The first time the children do this exercise, observe with which hand they choose to draw and with which eye they follow the movement. This will give you vital information about their dominant eye and hand. (See *A Guide to Child Health* by Michaela Glöckler and Wolfgang Goebel for more information on right/left dominance issues.)

The next time you do this exercise, instruct the students to use their right eye and right hand (except for those with true left dominance). Later, you could have your class close both eyes and draw the shape in the air with their hand, asking them to follow the movement of their hand with their closed eyes.

The forms, or letters, can be drawn on butcher paper on the floor of your classroom, allowing the children to make huge letters with their hands and their feet. Observe carefully, as this is the time to catch malformed letters early.

Pair the students, having one child write a letter on the other's back while saying the letter aloud. Then switch so that each gets a turn to experience both writing and feeling the letter. Later, you can have the children who have experienced the letter on their backs write the letter on paper or even say it aloud.

The letter is drawn on practice paper and, finally, when the children have really mastered it, they can draw it in their main lesson books.

Teaching Uppercase and Lowercase Letters

Because writing with a strictly uppercase script is a highly defensive method of writing, I suggest teaching the uppercase and lowercase letters at the same time. Here is an image of the uppercase writer: The uppercase letters are blocks, or bricks, circling the writer, preventing much from entering or being expressed. I know the uppercase letters are usually introduced first and that what I am saying goes against the traditional method of teaching in the Waldorf schools. Breaking the introduction of letters into small steps for the students is important, but the use of uppercase letters by themselves is not a desirable form of writing; it is something we don't want to encourage young children to practice.

Here is an example from my own life that illustrates my point about uppercase printing. When first studying the Vimala Alphabet, one of my classmates used printed uppercase letters exclusively. He spoke only when spoken to, and then only very softly. About three weeks later, we were in another class together. He was an altogether different person. He had decided the time was right for a big change and completely changed his writing to using the Vimala Alphabet, including both uppercase and lowercase letters, even connecting most of the letters. He went out to lunch with the class, was talkative, and shared fascinating stories about his life and his plans for the future. He had become a completely different person, now open and friendly, after only three weeks of dropping his uppercase writing.

If you do choose to present the uppercase letters first, I strongly urge you to introduce the lowercase letters as soon as possible. From that point on, please insist on writing that contains both uppercase and lowercase letters together through out the school years.

Connectivity

The Vimala Alphabet is a discontinuous style of cursive writing. Some of the letters reach out to join the next letter, but not all of them. Many of the uppercase, or capital letters, are actually printed and do not connect to the next letter. Cursive writing, or running style, connects the letters, and it is important to connect many, but not all the letters. Just as we reach out to others in friendship and community, our letters need to reach out to connect. However, if every letter is connected, there is no room for something new to enter. Imagine a group of people standing together. If there is no reaching out or holding hands (connecting strokes), there is little sense of community. Moreover, when everyone is holding hands, with no breaks (every stroke connected), there is no place for new people to join in or for new ideas to enter the circle. The connections can become fixed and stagnate. Space between letters allows for something new to come into our lives. After every five letters, leave a little space, or at least pick up your pen, so that there is not a string of six or more letters connected without a break of some kind.

Some letters, including many of the uppercase letters, lend themselves naturally to leaving spaces around them, because they begin in the upper zone. Some letters are best not connected to the letter before it; these include the *g, y, v, s, p* and *c*, because they begin at the waistline. The letter *k* starts in the upper zone with an "I am" stroke and does not connect to the letter before it. *X* and *x* always stand alone, not connected to any letter.

Writing Position

From day one, it is well worth the time spent to encourage the development of a relaxed grip when writing. When a child cradles the writing instrument in the hand, with the pencil resting on the curved middle finger and gently held between the base of the index finger and the thumb, it can be gripped without developing a white-knuckle approach. There are excellent pencil grips on the market to help establish a relaxed hold on the pen or pencil.

The tips of the fingers and thumb contain nerve endings that need to be stimulated when writing. Children enjoy hearing about how the thumb and first two fingers are friends that need to share, and so must all be close together when writing, and, of course, this encourages the proper position for holding the writing instrument.

Having the right size chair and desk for each student quickly turns into a huge challenge for teachers. Here are words of encouragement to help you persist in the effort. Have you tried sitting at a table that does not allow you to rest your arms comfortably on it, or sitting on a chair where your feet are forced to dangle in the air? The body becomes uncomfortable, which brings a degree of strenuousness to the task at hand. In order to write enjoyably, the knees of the child need to be slightly higher than the hips. The elbow should hang slightly lower than the top of the desk, and both feet need to rest flat on some surface. Foot-long pieces of 4 x 4 (or 2 x 4) wood can be placed on the floor, on which to rest the feet and achieve the correct alignment for feet, hips, and knees.

Children who bend over and place their face close to the paper when they write should have thier vision checked. They may have a vision problem, which adds to the frustration of writing. If vision is not the problem, then focus on good posture. Give your students the visualization of a rope along their spine. Ask them to feel it pulling up, as if they are puppets, until their head becomes erect. You can remind them, "No vultures at the desk," to encourage upright posture.

Writing Instruments

In Waldorf schools, the first letters are drawn with a colored pencil in the first grade, moving to pen in the third grade. Third or Fourth grade is a great time to introduce the goose feather quill. You can easily find these in public parks with ponds, at farms, or on the internet. See resources in the appendix (page 114) on how to harden the quill before cutting it at an angle with a sharp knife to form the writing tip. Learning to write beautifully with a quill requires patience and practice, both valuable skills worth cultivating. Making and writing with a quill pen is a rewarding and unforgettable experience to share with your class.

Using the Vimala Alphabet with Your Class

As the teacher, you must assess what is most needed to bring balance to your students. A class full of analytical minds might be guided to use more soft curves and arcades in their writing, which will bring feeling qualities to the forefront. A class that lives mostly in the feeling life could be taught to write with more angles to encourage intellectual faculties. For example, the letters *M*, *N* and *W* each have two forms, one more angled and the other more curved. It will be up to you to decide which forms to present and teach to your class.

In addition to using this alphabet as a way of writing, it can also be used as a tool to help bring balance to individual children. Each letter can be used to strengthen a quality, build up what is missing, or balance what is overactive, thus supporting healthy soul development. In Part three, after I share the quality of each letter, I also share some examples of when this letter might be useful for you, as the teacher, to help your class or a certain child overcome a hindrance. A particularly rebellious class, for instance, might spend more time with the letter *K* to support right relationship to authority.

In lectures, Steiner referred to teaching the students cursive in the first grade. The Vimala Alphabet is a print script well-suited for introducing the first letters young children learn. If you have already taught printing in the first grade, it is easy to introduce the Vimala Alphabet in second grade as your class's first connected form of writing.

If you have already introduced a cursive style of writing to your class, the Vimala Alphabet can be presented as a more modern style of writing in the later grades. There are teachers who present cursive writing, printing, and calligraphy, all in the first three grades. The Vimala Alphabet could be taught instead of any one of these.

Some teachers in the upper grades teach a "refresher" section on handwriting, in which all of the letters are practiced. This could be an opportunity to present a more modern style of writing to your class. To polish their handwriting skills, use this as a time to have them complete a practice sheet from part five for each letter of the alphabet.

In the upper grades especially, you could introduce the Vimala Alphabet through your personal handwriting changes, as seen by the class on the blackboard. I suggest simply using the Vimala Alphabet yourself in writing. When your class notices that your writing has changed, this could be the time to speak about the Vimala Alphabet.

As a teacher presenting the Vimala Alphabet to your class, I strongly recommend a program of practicing your own handwriting before presenting this style to your class. It is important to develop an intuitive understanding of the letters before presenting them. Just like any other aspect of the curriculum, allow it to live in you first. With a copy of the Vimala Alphabet in front of you, practice each letter and feel how different it feels from your usual way of writing. Some letters you may already form like the Vimala Alphabet, some changes may be easy to make. The changes that are hardest to make will bring you the most benefit. (See Vimala Rodgers's excellent book, *Your Handwriting Can Change Your Life,* on adults changing their handwriting.)

Child Study

Observing a child's handwriting as we would the child's movements can reveal valuable information and offer insight about the child. These insights can be used during the child study portion of a faculty meeting to help find a creative remedy when a difficult situation arises. Consider, too, the first letter of the first name; it can summarize the opportunity (or challenge) each of us face in life, while the first letter of the last name points to our work in the world. A program of specific handwriting changes can produce real shifts in a person, young or old.

Part Two: Terms of Art

Before we can begin our study of the letters, there are a few basic concepts and terms that will assist us in grasping the subject. While the quality of the letters is paramount, there are a few strokes worth mentioning here.

Zones

Letters are written in three different zones:

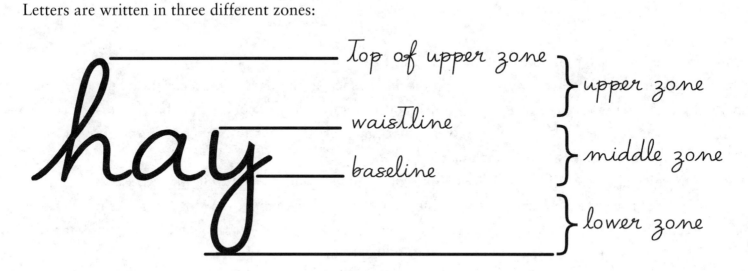

The zones compare to the parts of the human body. The upper zone, the area of the head, shows us our connection to thoughts, philosophies, and the spiritual world. The middle zone, where the heart, lungs, and digestion live, relates to our everyday life. The lower zone speaks of our actions, relationships, and the need for movement and change.

The "baseline" is the imaginary line on which we write (or, with lined paper, reveals the actual line on which you write), the bottom of the middle zone. The straightness or wavering nature of this line reveals our general outlook on life. A baseline that rises as it crosses the page speaks of optimism, whereas one that falls tells of a more pessimistic attitude. Many letters begin at the baseline, a centered and grounded place to start, while others begin at the top of the upper zone, bringing the gifts from Heaven to Earth.

The dividing line between the middle zone and the bottom of the upper zone is called the "waistline."

Many teachers use the handwriting practice books developed by Else Gottgens, a master teacher and mentor from Holland. These are widely available from Waldorf supply channels and show the zones through pink and green bars of color. You can use these books to guide students in developing the letters within the correct zones.

Margins

There are four margins: top, bottom, left, and right. Each tells us a great deal.

The top margin expresses how we relate to authority. In fact, in the days of queens and kings, one would not have dared to write in the top half of the page when addressing royalty, out of fear of showing disrespect. This is, of course, no longer necessary. Nevertheless, a very small top margin shows resistance to authority. A healthy top margin is about one inch on an 8½ x 11 inch page.

The left margin represents the past and where we are coming from; the right margin represents the future and where we are going. The past is important, but we must put it behind us to move into the future. I suggest a one-inch margin on the left and right, although I would not discourage children from going as far right as possible *without* hitting the edge of the page or border. It is our children's birthright to live into the future.

The bottom margin shows our relationship to aesthetics. I suggest a healthy minimum of one inch for the bottom margin on an 8½ x 11 inch page.

Page Orientation

In the main lesson books, it is easiest to write, whether right-handed or left-handed, with the page oriented in the "landscape" direction, with the stitching at the top of the page. This direction allows creative "out of the box" thinking, something that will become increasingly valuable in the future. When we write with the page turned in the traditional "portrait" direction, we support the status quo and conformity. Using main lesson books in the landscape direction greatly supports the creative thinking we associate with Waldorf education.

When writing all the way across the main lesson page presents a challenge for students, check to see whether there is a midline issue. Hold your finger or other object at eye level, and ask them to follow it with their eyes as you move it back and forth, from right to left and left to right, very slowly. If their eyes flicker when the object crosses their nose, have them practice "running forms" (*eeeee* and *ellellelle*) to help relieve this situation. First, start with big forms on the board, then on large sheets of paper. Follow all of the steps in the exercises section in part one. Make sure that the child is standing with his or her center facing the work surface. Watch to make sure the child crosses the midline while engaged in any of these activities, as there is a tendency to avoid this movement. Any activity at the midline will also be helpful, such as kneading dough.

Baseline

For the beginning writer, a blank page can seem large and overwhelming. Else Gottgens' practice book for handwriting displays the zones in different colors. Using green and pink bars of colors to guide the child to draw the correct size for the upper, middle, and lower zones, these practice books are highly recommended to assist children in learning to write in the early grades. Once children have gained some confidence with the sizes of the different zones, they can move onto the unlined page.

When first using blank paper, the children can draw a line across the page using the "Mama Bear" side (the small side) of their block crayons as a guide. Use the top of this line as the baseline and place the lower zone of the letters within the bar of color.

We can give children guidelines (literally) by placing a liner under the writing paper. A liner is a page with lines representing the baseline that are bold enough to be visible through the writing paper. A liner can assist children in developing their own baseline over time. *The length of time it will take children to write with a straight baseline by themselves will vary tremendously.* Use a liner only as long as necessary. As soon as they are able to create a straight baseline on their own, eliminate the liner.

The ideal is to have the children write with a straight baseline on unlined paper in the landscape direction, without the help of lines. When you encourage your class to write on unlined paper, you support the children in becoming creative, trailblazing human beings. The unlined page asks children to create the basis for their life out of themselves. In creating the baseline on their own, they develop inner strength and self-guidance through this effort.

Slant

Here is an analogy between slant and body language: Think of sitting next to another person and having a conversation. When the person leans very slightly toward you, it creates closeness that is conducive to talking and sharing. When someone leans deeply in your direction, it can be overwhelming. Yet, when the person leans backward, away from you, it can be a challenge to maintain a conversation. It is the same with the slant of writing.

The slant of our writing shows where we stand on the spectrum of emotions. Writing that slants to the far right shows reactivity and an emotional life that overwhelms the personality. It speaks of one who is so emotional that individual expression cannot be controlled. The more upright the slant, the more control we display over our feelings and their expression. I suggest a predominantly upright slant in writing, with only a slight (five-degree) slant to the right. This speaks of a feeling person who has control over the emotions. Those who slant their writing to the left armor and withhold themselves and should be encouraged gently to lean the letters toward the right, leading to a more upright slant.

Pressure

The amount of pressure one applies to the pen and paper speaks of the enthusiasm, vitality, and the investment one pours into life. The harder the pressure, the more intense the personality. Be aware of the child who has an overly tight grasp on the writing instrument; this is a very difficult habit to break and can interfere with the child's enjoyment of writing. A pencil grip, a small plastic piece that covers the area where the fingers touch the writing instrument, can be used to help children who hold on too tightly.

Spacing

When the letters are quite close, it looks as though the student has trouble breathing and shows a person with limited self-expression. Watch as the child writes; is the hand and shoulder relaxed? Encourage more space between the letters to display an openness and free expression of the self.

In terms of spacing between the words, ideally, the space required to write the lowercase letter "a" is the correct amount of space to leave between words. When the words are closer than this, in addition to being difficult to read, it shows a person who depends on being surrounded by others all the time. When words are very widely spaced, there may be a need to pause and reflect before assimilating events or ideas. It could also tell us that the writer needs to keep others at a distance to feel safe.

The space between the lines of writing reveals mental clarity and sense of order. The lines should be far enough apart so that the upper zone of one line does not get tangled in the lower zone from the line above. Letters tangled together show disorganization and a lack of clarity. Lines that are very widely spaced indicates one who thinks things need to be "just so," one who gets upset with the unexpected and who places excessive value on structure and planning.

For those who need a little help with line spacing, use a liner as described in the section on baselines. The use of a liner can encourage the young writer to space lines so that they are close, but not overlapping. Make sure that the spaces between the lines of the liner allow ample room for the size of the writing. Liners are easy to make, or they can be purchased with various widths between lines.

Tie Strokes

A statement of perseverance, tie strokes say, "Nothing will stop me." A tie stroke first crosses to the left of the vertical stroke, then forms a small loop, and finally crosses back over the vertical stroke. Once this stroke crosses back over the vertical line, it says, "I place the outcome in God's/Spirit's hands; I am unattached to the results." If any one element described here is missing from this three-part formula, it is not a tie stroke. Tie strokes, or persistence strokes, display a commitment and drive to completion. These highly desirable strokes occur in the *A*, *g*, *H*, and *f*.

"I am" Strokes

This stroke is a simple vertical line, as in the uppercase *I*. It starts at the top of the upper zone and ends at the baseline. Children enjoy remembering to use this stroke to bring the gifts from Heaven down to use here in our earthly home. The "I am" stroke is found in many uppercase letters and in some lowercase letters. This stroke should be made at a five-degree slant.

Garlands

This soft, playful stroke is on the baseline and looks like a hand reaching out to join hands with another. We find it providing connectivity at the end of many letters. Use the garland generously, but be careful not join every letter, as we need some space between the letters to allow intuition to enter our lives. This stroke is found at the end of many of the lower case letters.

Arcades

Arcades, like garlands, are soft curves, but they begin at the baseline, head upward, and then curve down again. It is best not to retrace the downward part of arcades when the stroke heads back up toward the waistline, otherwise an "it has always been done this way" kind of attitude can slip in. Arcades are found in the letters *m, n,* and *h.*

Bridge Strokes

A bridge stroke is a small stroke that connects letters, usually at the waistline. This type of connecting stroke is used for letters whose final stroke ends at the waistline, such as *o* and *w.*

Lincoln's Foot

This introductory stroke, named after Abraham Lincoln, begins the letters *A, M,* and *N.* This stroke brings qualities of playfulness and warm humor and reinforces our desire to reach out to others in true community.

Retracing Strokes

When forming the letters, there are two basic guidelines to follow: one for strokes that lead into the upper zone (upstrokes), and one for strokes that head downward to the baseline (downstrokes). It is important to retrace the upstrokes, such as in the stems of the letters *d* and *t.* It is equally important *not* to retrace downstrokes in letters such as *m, n,* and *h,* and in the stems of *B, b, D, F, K, k, P, p,* and *R.* (See each letter for additional details on retracing strokes.)

Printing

Printing and, even more so, block printing (using all uppercase letters) are forms of protective writing. Intuitively, one senses that, when we print, we are actually sharing less of ourselves than when we write cursive. Encourage students who print to transition to cursive by having them reach out and connect some letters with garlands and bridge strokes. In addition, present "running forms" as form drawings and borders with circular shapes, which can also help these children. Children who always print tend to have established protective barriers for some reason and need gentle encouragement to remove them.

If you have a student who block prints, encourage the child to first add some lowercase printed letters and then, later, move to connecting the letters. This type of writing speaks of someone who has felt serious wounding in life. Please be gentle and encourage such children to make changes slowly.

Part Three: The Letters

In this section, I introduce each of the letters, their qualities, how they can bring balance, and details on how to form them. The qualities of the letters are contained in both the uppercase and lowercase forms. Quotes from Rudolf Steiner's *Eurythmy as Visible Speech* are included to give a fuller picture of the nature of the letters. Please note that, in this work, he refers to the spoken, not the written, letters.

The Vowels

$$A a \quad E \varrho \varepsilon \quad I i \quad O o \quad U u$$

The vowels carry the feelings and inner soul stirrings. These singing sounds form the basic building blocks of our communication. We can hear this in the emotional qualities of speech from an adolescent—"I dUnnO." It is mostly vowel sounds! Vowels form the basis for conveying feeling and intent. Consonants wrap themselves around the vowels, giving form and structure.

Teaching the vowels is most effectively presented at a time of heightened consciousness. Because the vowels express the inner world of the soul, teaching them to your class when the forces of the Earth are most active, such as during Advent, will support learning. While the outer world sleeps, the inner life experiences its most fruitful time. During this time of inner activity, present what you most wish to bring forth in the children. Teaching the alphabet, especially the vowels, during the Advent season helps give rise to ensouled language in your class.

The vowels are best presented and characterized through physical gesture, image, and the mood of the vowel. If possible, use the eurythmy gestures for the vowel sounds in your introduction of the vowels. The consonants are best presented in an artistic way through pictures and stories.

Later on, when the students begin to spell, it will be very helpful if you have included in your presentation both the short and long sounds of each vowel.

The Letter *A*:

A a

QUALITY: When we write the letter *A*, it expresses the human being at the "highest perfection, expressing something that is felt in the depths of the human soul," says Rudolf Steiner of the spoken sound "ah" in his book, *Eurythmy as Visible Speech*. Forming the letter *A* as illustrated shows our ability to stand, truth-filled and free of judgment. Using this healthy form of writing allows us to take the center stage without being egotistical and to share what we know, without generating harm to anyone.

SUPPORTING SOUL DEVELOPMENT: *A* is the perfect letter for the child who is uncomfortable being on stage and the center of attention. Those students who hesitate to raise their hand receive tremendous support from this letter; they can get up in the front of the class to give a presentation or be center-stage in a performance.

It is also helpful for children who love being center stage and who want the focus to be only on them. This letter can bring such a quality into a more balanced relationship, helping children to realize that their part is important, but not the whole show.

FORMATION OF THE LETTER: The uppercase letter begins with a sweeping Lincoln's foot, heads to a point at the top of the upper zone and heads back to the baseline with a down stroke slightly slanted to the left (this last stroke is the "I am" stroke). Once it touches the baseline, it retraces the down stroke very briefly and forms a tie stroke to the left, first heading up, then crossing the beginning stroke and curving down and back to cross over the "I am" stroke.

The lowercase *a* begins at the waistline with an oval, then reaches out to meet the next letter in a small garland.

The Letter *Ɛ:*

Ɛ ℓ ε

QUALITY: The letter *Ɛ* points to the level of compassion and tolerance we display in the world. "The freed individuality within the community of souls—a coming together with the other," as Steiner puts it. A narrow, pinched lowercase *ℓ* may show little tolerance for the opinions or feelings of others. In handwriting, the letter *ℓ* expresses the ability to listen to others as we would like others to listen to us. There are two forms of lowercase *Ɛ*. The "teardrop" *ℓ* is most commonly used. Less common is the epsilon *ε*, which is used to help develop literary interest or talent.

SUPPORTING SOUL DEVELOPMENT: Do you have students who are critical of people who make choices different from their own? This is the letter to practice, using the Vimala Alphabet form to develop a more accepting attitude.

Do you have a student with poor literary skills? Do you see writing talent that you view as a real gem, and you want to see it developed? Encourage the use of the epsilon *ε* to cultivate literary talent in either case.

FORMATION OF THE LETTER: The uppercase *Ɛ* begins at the top of the upper zone, sweeping left into a loop to the waistline, and then making a second slightly larger loop to the left, ending with a slight upswing at the baseline.

The lowercase *ℓ* is formed by starting at the baseline, swinging to the right, curving backward at the waistline, forming a full and open loop, and ending at the baseline with a slight upswing. The lowercase literary elipson *ε* starts at the waistline and copies the shape of the uppercase *Ɛ*.

The Letter *I* :

I i

QUALITY: How we shape the letter *I* tells us how clearly we see, especially in the present moment. Are we present to the "here and now"? Do we see the world and ourselves clearly or is our perception clouded by illusions?

SUPPORTING SOUL DEVELOPMENT: Do you have a student who is dreamy, lost in thinking about what happened yesterday or looking forward to the weekend? To bring your students more into the present moment, help them dot the *i* directly on top. Do you have a student who embellishes the facts or is unable recall a situation accurately? Look at the letter *i* and practice this form to bring more clarity.

When the *i* looks as though it is doing the splits (the upstroke and the downstroke wide apart), it can show that a child is rigid. To help create flexibility, have the student retrace the upstroke, parting the strokes only at the baseline.

FORMATION OF THE LETTER: To write the letter *I*, begin with an "I am" stroke by starting at the top of the upper zone with a slightly slanting (five-degree) stroke to the baseline. Next, place a cross stroke slanted upward at the top of the "I am" stroke. Finish this letter off with a straight line at the baseline.

The lowercase letter begins at the baseline and reaches to the waistline, then retraces the stroke until it reaches the baseline once again forming the stem of the letter. It ends with a garland reaching out to the next letter. Be sure to dot your *i* close to the top of the stem. Be aware of "flying" dots. Dotting your *i* to the left of the stem reveals someone lost in thought about the past, just as one placed to the right shows someone thinking about the future. An *i* dotted directly above the stem speaks of being present in the here and now, just where one belongs.

The Letter O:

O o

QUALITY: The letter O is part of the communication family of letters, as are all the lowercase letters that have an oval in the middle zone. The shape of the letter O tells us of one's ability to speak from a compassionate and understanding place. It helps us develop the ability to speak to the listening of the other, speaking the truth in a way that can be heard. As Dr. Vimala Rodgers says, "To tell a dull person that he is stupid may be factual, but it is also cruel. Truth on its highest level never harms, justifies, or defends." In *Eurythmy as Visible Speech*, Rudolf Steiner says about the spoken letter O, "We feel not only ourselves, but also reach beyond to feel something else or another being whom we want to embrace."

SUPPORTING SOUL DEVELOPMENT: Do you have a chatty child in class? Have the child close the letter o so that there is no break in the oval. You may be surprised to see how much more work gets done with less talking. The opposite is also true; having children expand a compressed o will help them become talkative.

This letter also works well for choleric children who don't see how much their speech hurts others. By practicing writing this letter, one's speech can become more sensitive to the listener. Practice this letter to develop language skills filled with compassion.

FORMATION OF THE LETTER: We want to see the O shaped as an oval, free from loops or clutter of any kind; clutter inside of the O represents things we hide, maybe even from ourselves!

The uppercase and lowercase letters are formed the same, except for size. The uppercase letter fills the upper and middle zones with an oval shape. The lowercase letter fills just the middle zone and may have a bridge stroke extending it to meet the next letter.

The Letter *U*:

Uu

QUALITY: The shape of the letter *U* speaks of our receptivity, openness to learning, and an ability to hear the opinions of others. The essence of the letter *U* is similar to the goal of the fifth of the Six Basic Exercises by Rudolf Steiner, who said it "allows the union with the universal to be reached."

SUPPORTING SOUL DEVELOPMENT: If our strong opinions don't allow other information to enter, practicing writing the letter *u* will cultivate openness to new ideas, methods, and approaches. Have you ever had students who act as if they know everything and will not let anyone else get a word in edgewise? By practicing the letter *u*, such students might be able to say, "I may be wrong." It can soften the hardest choleric temperament.

FORMATION OF THE LETTER: The uppercase letter starts at the top of the upper zone and heads straight down to the baseline where it curves back into the upper zone, this time not quite as high. Then it heads back to the baseline again, ending with a sweet garland reaching out to the next letter. The lowercase *u* is made exactly the same way, except it lives only within the middle zone, starting and ending between the baseline and the waistline.

Notice how the cup shape of the *U* is slightly shorter on the right. This is an important aspect of this letter; it is almost as if we are filled with understanding and allow it to spill out for the benefit of others.

The Consonants

Bb Cc Dd Ff Gg Hh Jj Kk Ll MMm
NNn Pp Qq Rr Ss TT Vv WWww Xx Yy Zz

Like the sides of the riverbank that define the path and flow of the river, the shaping sounds of consonants give form and structure. In Waldorf schools, the consonants are introduced through images that incorporate the shapes and sounds of the letters. For example, the letter G becomes a goose looking over her shoulder, with the second, separate stroke forming the wing. In this way, the shape of the letter, its sound, and the image all convey the letter G. Now to incorporate one more element: place the goose on a nest of golden eggs. Loved and honored for the treasure she provides, the goose now carries one of the qualities of the letter G: prosperity. These four elements (shape, sound, image, and quality), woven together, create a powerful message for the young child.

Because the letters each express a specific quality, the most important consideration is to select an image that is meaningful for you; you will convey it to your class. Earlier I mentioned using *cat* for the letter C, *king* for K, and a lovable *prince* with arms outstretched for P. These examples use the form of the letter, a picture, and a sound, together with the soul qualities of each letter.

Consider the soul economy of presenting the letters with positive moral or aesthetic qualities. Rudolf Steiner, for example, presented the word *bath* for B to encourage cleanliness. Keep in mind what would be most beneficial for your class when selecting images for each of the letters.

The Letter *B* :

B b

QUALITY: The shape of this letter contains a protecting and sheltering form. It shows valuing community, especially spirit-centered community, in which everyone benefits without any losers. It not only values self and the other, it is also the living expression in the world of such caring.

SUPPORTING SOUL DEVELOPMENT: Children often put themselves first when dealing with others, rather than working for the mutual good of all concerned. To plant the seeds of developing community as the child matures, use the letter *b*. For the child who somehow always ends up holding the short end of the stick, this is also the letter to practice.

FORMATION OF THE LETTER: The *B* starts with an "I am" stroke, beginning in the upper zone and ending at the baseline. Then lift the pen and begin at the top again, just to the left of the "I am" stroke, to form a small reverse c shape on top and another larger reverse c shape on the bottom, swinging the stroke past the "I am" stroke and bringing it forward, ending with it leading into the future (to the right). It is very important that the upper loop of the *B* is smaller than the lower loop, which balances the needs of others with one's own needs.

Start the lowercase *b* with an "I am" stroke, then lift the pen. Form an oval headed to the right, making sure it is closed at the bottom, and ending with a stroke to the right that reaches out to the next letter.

The Letter C:

C c

QUALITY: A seemingly simple shape, this letter is difficult to make without hooks and loops. This makes sense when we realize that this letter represents complete trust and our willingness to be vulnerable. Or, as Steiner puts it, "the condition of being light."

Most of us don't live in complete trust, so it is easy to understand the challenge of perfecting this letter. We can all cultivate a more trusting approach to life, knowing that everything happens for a reason. We may not know why, even after reflection later on, but we can trust that there is a cosmic order in life and recognize that we have our small role in it.

SUPPORTING SOUL DEVELOPMENT: For those children who wish to be different than they are, or for those who struggle with one subject and feel inferior because of it, this is the letter to practice. For the child who misses Mom and Dad every day at school or who worries excessively, this letter, done correctly, can help bring peace and acceptance. For those children who do not feel safe, practicing the letter C will help restore confidence that they will be cared for.

FORMATION OF THE LETTER: The uppercase letter C begins at the top of the upper zone and makes a wide swing to the left and down to the baseline. The lowercase letter is made the same way starting at the waistline, ending at the baseline. There are no hooks, loops, or introductory strokes to this letter.

The Letter *Ð* :

Ð d

QUALITY: The shape of this letter in its highest form expresses sensitivity to others, while maintaining kind, clear boundaries. In its lowest form, this letter can express a personal sense of inadequacy through being too concerned with what others think, as well as an inability to confront others, which can lead to speech that lacks directness. *Ð* reminds us that it is truly none of our business what other people think about us; their opinions reveal more about them than they do us. *Ð* speaks of who I am in the world.

SUPPORTING SOUL DEVELOPMENT: Reactivity best describes what this letter heals. It supports the ability to stop being at the mercy of outer events, as a leaf in the wind, blown hither and yon. It allows one to respond out of choice to the surrounding activity. This letter also helps develop skills to handle the challenge of confrontation.

Use this letter with great success for children who are overly eager for people to like them, as well as for those who are insensitive to the feelings of others. Use this letter with the sensitive shy type, or those who want greater closeness with others but fear getting hurt if they reach out.

Watch for loops in the stem of the lowercase *d*. The "d looper" will tend to be reactive and emotional, focusing more on others' opinions and not minding one's own business.

FORMATION OF THE LETTER: The uppercase *Ð* begins with an "I am" stroke; the second stroke begins to the left of the "I am" stroke and forms a reverse *c*, crossing back over the "I am" stroke and looping forward to the right. The letter *Ð* is "full-bodied"; it should not be a slim letter.

Lowercase *d* begins at the waistline, forms an oval and then heads straight up to the top of the upper zone. It is of utmost importance that it retraces the stroke exactly (no loops in the stem), ending at the baseline with a garland reaching out to the next letter.

The Letter *F*:

F f

QUALITY: *F* is one of my favorite letters, because it has worked so powerfully in my life. Its shape speaks of expressing our talents fully in the world without attachment to the results.

The shape of the letter *f* says, "I am grounded. I have my own ideas and creative impulses, which I vigorously give in service to the world. I offer my contributions as a gift. Nothing will stop me; I have given it my all, and I am unattached to the results." Steiner describes it this way, as "consciousness being permeated with wisdom" and "know that I know."

Everyone comes into the world with work to do, or "dharma," as the yogis would call it. This letter helps us find our work and take it into the world, living it fully without attachment to the results. At age fifty, this letter has helped me to discover my life's work. The "triple looper" *f* brings clarity to gifts and talents, helping to launch them into reality. When you introduce it to your class you support them in finding clarity about their work and creativity in the world early in life.

SUPPORTING SOUL DEVELOPMENT: Do you have students who lack confidence and cannot see the gifts they bring? Or children who tend to put others first, at their own expense? Or a those who cannot quite bring a project to completion; they are almost finished, then things fall apart? The phlegmatic child can also receive some get-up-and-go from practicing this letter. The letter *f* can assist all of these children.

FORMATION OF THE LETTER: The uppercase F is printed, whereas the lowercase f starts at the baseline, sweeps up to the top of the upper zone, forming a loop, then heads down into the lower zone with a vertical stroke. In the lower zone, a healthy loop (two times the height of the midzone) is made, then the stroke heads up to the baseline. On the left of the vertical stroke, form a small loop (tie stroke) just above the baseline and once again cross over the vertical stroke, ending with slight upstroke to the right.

The lowercase f is the only lowercase letter to occupy all three zones. Although challenging to develop, the results of forming this letter correctly are well worth the effort.

Make sure your students form the tie stroke on the left side of the vertical line. The loop does not qualify as a tie stroke unless the loop starts and closes to the left of the vertical line.

The Letter G :

G g

QUALITY: This letter, both the uppercase and the lowercase forms, speaks of our degree of ease in working with others. It also expresses gratitude in receiving. Because the lowercase g reaches into the lower zone, it also displays our determination to get the job done. The letter G could be summed up as the letter of prosperity.

SUPPORTING SOUL DEVELOPMENT: What a letter! It expresses gratitude, ease in working with others, determination, positivity. This important letter ignites the ability to bring what we want into our lives now. Enjoy its grace and beauty as it flows from the middle zone to the lower zone and back again. Encourage your students to practice this letter when there is difficulty getting along with others, inadequate determination to follow through to get the job done, or an "Eyore" (heightened melancholic) attitude.

FORMATION OF THE LETTER: The uppercase G is the only letter composed of two separate, never touching, strokes. There is no place for angles in the letter G; keep all lines soft and curvy. Begin with a basic uppercase C, next, write a straight line, starting in the middle of the C form and curving to end, just above the baseline. Remember, no touching these two lines.

The lowercase g begins with a c, then sweeps down into the lower zone to form a loop about two times the height of the midzone, ending with a slight upstroke to the right in the midzone ready to connect to the next letter.

The Letter *H*:

H h

QUALITY: Steiner says that this letter is midway between a vowel and a consonant. A well formed *H* represents an expression of one's passion in life lived fully, without holding back. Wow, a life lived fully! That must be why the founder of this alphabet has practiced a full page of the letter *H h* everyday for more than twenty years. This letter also contains the qualities of honoring others and expressing it.

SUPPORTING SOUL DEVELOPMENT: This letter helps phlegmatic children who ask why they should get out of bed in the morning. It helps restore the drive to live life fully every day, loving every minute.

Have you ever had students who are deeply afraid of their own unique gifts or capacities? The Vimala *h* is the exact letter to practice for these children to give them courage. Look for a letter *h* that changes direction of the stroke and moves to the left (*h*) and help any child change this undesirable form.

FORMATION OF THE LETTER: The Uppercase *H* is formed with two "I am" strokes. From the second "I am" stroke, the pen is drawn to the left looping over the first "I am" stroke, forming a tie stroke and ending with a curve at the waistline.

The lowercase *h* starts at the baseline, heads up into the upper zone forming an *l*, returns to the baseline in a narrow *v* shape, then heads back up to the waistline in an arcade that ends at the baseline, reaching out to the next letter. Be sure this letter forms a *v* shape at the baseline and does not pull back just before reaching out to meet the next letter.

There are only three lowercase letters that have a loop in the upper zone: *h, l,* and *f*. Any other loops in the upper zone in the lowercase letters are not desirable.

The Letter *J*:

J j

QUALITY: Working with the letter *J* helps us to listen to the voice within, our intuition. It helps us develop our sense of inner knowing what is right and wrong for us in each moment. It strengthens our intuition so that we feel more connected to others and understand them better.

SUPPORTING SOUL DEVELOPMENT: Have you ever wished you had followed that little voice inside of you that whispered, "That's a great idea," or other guidance? Practice the letter *j* and experience how that whisper can turn into a loud and clear message. Our children also need to strengthen their inner voice so they can more easily distinguish right from wrong. It helps children who are passing through a lying stage to practice the letter *J*. This letter can help us to see circumstances clearly, allowing us to perceive our personal involvement instead of being blind to it.

FORMATION OF THE LETTER: To form the uppercase letter *J*, begin just below the baseline with a sweeping stroke to the top of the upper zone; after curving down, it heads straight down into the lower zone. Here it makes a smaller loop and returns to the baseline. A small *v* shape is formed out of the beginning stroke and the ending stroke crossing at the baseline.

The lowercase *j* begins at the baseline with a sweeping stroke to the waistline, then it drops into the lower zone with a loop one-and-a-half times the height of the midzone, returning to the baseline with a stroke that reaches out to the next letter.

The Letter K :

K k

QUALITY: Within the shape of the letter K comes our knowledge of when to lead and when to follow, our relationship to authority. *Authority* is an powerful word; it comes from the word "to author." In the U.S. in the twenty-first century, *authority* has earned a bad reputation. We want our children to be free thinkers, so shouldn't we start the students with freedom from the very beginning? When children are given appropriate role models of people who author their own lives, they can develop their own authority later in life.

It is sad to see children given too many choices too early, because it creates insecurity for little ones, who are unprepared to make decisions. The classic example of this is well-meaning parents offering their children too many choices for breakfast: "Do you want eggs for breakfast—fried or soft-boiled or an omelet with cheese and herbs or only herbs? Do you want toast with that—with butter or with jam?" and so on, endlessly. It is far kinder to children to offer two choices: "Do you want eggs or oatmeal for breakfast?" They will feel safe, knowing that someone is in charge, and not feel the burden of responsibility for making so many decisions. When given this kind of guidance early on, later in life they will be confident enough to choose freely, out of a secure center, because as young people they developed a strong sense of their own authority. (See Penni Sparks' great work on Ennobled™ Parenting at www.pennisparks.com.)

SUPPORTING SOUL DEVELOPMENT: We have all experienced rebellious children. And, we do need the rebels! Have them practice the letter k and watch their rebellion take more appropriate forms, learning when it is time to lead and when it is time to follow. Use this letter for the rebels, as well as for those students who buckle under pressure.

FORMATION OF THE LETTER: Beginning with an "I am" stroke, the uppercase K has just two strokes. The second stroke begins at the top of the upper zone forming a sideways V that just touches but does *not* cross the "I am" stroke and ends at the baseline. Please have your students avoid crossing these lines!

The lowercase k also begins with an "I am" stroke. The second stroke begins at the waistline, forms a sideways V, and ends at the baseline. It is very important to have this second stroke of the lowercase letter occupy only the midzone.

Please remember there are no curves or loops in either the uppercase or lowercase k. All lines are straight in this letter.

The Letter 𝓛 :

𝓛 𝓁

QUALITY: This letter speaks of our innate spiritual nature and being true to our sence of truth. It contains elements of self-reflection and the recognition that spirit exists in all material substance. Steiner says it is, "the transforming of matter by form." Ideally, the 𝓁 occupies both upper zone and middle zone with a healthy loop.

SUPPORTING SOUL DEVELOPMENT: Waldorf education does a wonderful job with helping students stay in touch with the spiritual nature of life through celebrating the seasons, stories of fairies and gnomes, and acknowledgement of the seen and unseen.

When it is time for the dreamy child to wake up to material/physical existence here on Earth, or when a child lives too deeply in philosophical concepts and the intellect, look at the letter 𝓁. It may be too wide and open, or pinched tight. When children are uncomfortable with their actions, when they have compromised their own standards, have them practice this letter. If you have students who are prone to fantasizing, have them practice the Vimala 𝓁.

FORMATION OF THE LETTER: Form the uppercase 𝓛 by starting in the upper zone, make a slightly curved stroke up and to the left and then at a five-degree slant reaching down to the baseline. Here make a small loop to the left, returning to the baseline, ending with a slight upswing.

Lowercase 𝓁 starts at the baseline, swing the stroke up to the top of the upper zone, then with a narrow loop to the left end the stroke at the baseline, reaching out to the next letter.

NOTE: Don't completely throw away the old Palmer L (𝓛); use it to decorate the borders on the main lesson book pages and to calm the class. When connected into a long stream of 𝓛s, we call it "miles of lace," and it can be used to reverse the energy in the classroom. Try this after recess when the class has been out playing in the wind to settle things down and bring the class back into a focused, listening mood.

The Letter *M*:

M M m

QUALITY: This is the letter of Divine Grace. Or as Steiner put it, the letter *m* speaks of "a marvelous understanding of the universe." This letter also expresses the level of comfort we have in working one-on-one, in groups, and with humanity at large. It speaks to our level of grace in relationships.

SUPPORTING SOUL DEVELOPMENT: Do you have a student who embraces conformity rather than creativity? Since this letter shows our level of comfort with groups of people, any fears or blockages in relating to others can be released by perfecting the letter *m*. Fearful children will retrace the down strokes (*m*), pressing them together. Have them stretch the letter apart to help them experience divine grace.

FORMATION OF THE LETTER: There are two forms of this uppercase letter. The angular shape will stimulate more of the thinking faculties, whereas having your class use the curvy shapes will lead them to their feeling life. In forming the rounded uppercase *M*, where the upward and downward strokes meet at the bottom of the letter, you could make them even looser than shown here by forming a narrow *v* shape: *M*. As the teacher, you will need to decide which shape to introduce, depending on what would most benefit your class. It is always possible to introduce the other shape later, if that feels right.

The uppercase *M* begins with a playful introductory stroke. *M* starts at the top of the upper zone and heads down to the baseline. Without retracing the stroke just made, a narrow *v* is formed at the baseline. Next, it heads back to the top of the upper zone forming an arcade, then goes back down to the baseline, forming another narrow *v*, while heading back up for another arcade only slightly shorter, and finally down again to end at the baseline.

The *M* and *m* both flow like water gently cascading down, with the first arcade the largest and each arcade getting progressively shorter, never retracing the down stroke. Each time this letter touches the baseline it forms a narrow *v* instead of retracing the down stroke.

The angular uppercase *M* begins at the baseline with a sweeping Lincoln's foot (as in the letter *A*). It heads to the top of the upper zone, ends in a point, and heads to the baseline. Here it makes a soft point and heads to the upper zone, but not quite as high this time. It again forms a point in the upper zone and returns to the baseline with a garland reaching out to the next letter.

With the lowercase *m* beginning at the baseline, this letter heads to the waistline, forms an arcade and heads to the baseline again. Once at the baseline, it forms a narrow *v*, reaching up to the waistline forming another arcade, this one slightly smaller. This is repeated to form the third arcade, once again, smaller than the other two arcades.

The Letter *N* :

n N n

QUALITY: *n* speaks of being a loving, faithful friend, a good listener who gives from the heart. It is simple and playful, with the first arcade representing the self, the second arcade representing the other.

SUPPORTING SOUL DEVELOPMENT: Use this letter to help the child who has a hard time making friends or has a difficult time being a good friend to others. For the child who lives more in the head and would benefit from some playtime with others, this is the letter to practice. The letter *n* is lighthearted and fun; explore this letter to bring out these qualities.

FORMATION OF THE LETTER: Once again, based on the needs of your students, choose which form will best serve your class—the more intellectual, angular shape or the more feeling, curvy shape.

The uppercase *n* begins with a playful introductory stroke, starting at the top of the upper zone and heading down to the baseline. Without retracing the stroke just made and forming a narrow *v*, the stroke then heads back to the top of the upper zone, then heads back down to the baseline forming a garland reaching out to join with the next letter.

The angular uppercase *N* begins at the baseline with a sweeping, concave stroke to the top of the upper zone, where it ends in a point and heads to the baseline slightly angled to the right. Here it makes a *v* and heads with an arching stroke to the right, ending in the upper zone.

The lowercase *n*, like the *m*, begins at the baseline, and heads to the waistline, forms an arcade and heads to the baseline again. Once at the baseline and forming a narrow *v*, it reaches up to the waistline forming another arcade, this one slightly smaller. The trick for this letter is to never retrace the down stroke, instead forming a narrow *v* when this letter touches the baseline. When you retrace the down stroke, you reinforce fear.

The Letter *P*:

P p

QUALITY: The letter *P* speaks of self-love and how we feel about ourselves. When we feel loved and lovable, the need to argue, become angry, and be overly exact falls away, and our relationships magically improve.

SUPPORTING SOUL DEVELOPMENT: Ask children who are always critical of their work, no matter how beautiful, to practice this letter. For children who judge themselves harshly and who feel out of place, who can't seem to forgive a wrong, whether their own or someone else's—this is the letter to practice. Do you have a child who wants to please other people, and because his feeling of self-worth comes from the outside, he gets easily depressed? Do you have children who need to argue and are overly critical of others? Try the letter *p*.

FORMATION OF THE LETTER: The uppercase letter begins with an "I am" stroke starting in the upper zone. The second stroke starts at the top of the upper zone, forming a backward *c* to the waistline, and heads to the right crossing over (or at least touching) the "I am" stroke. It loops forward, ending right at the waistline or slightly above.

The lowercase *p* also begins with an "I am" stroke, but starting at the waistline and ending in the lower zone. The second stroke starts at the waistline, forms a backward *c* shape that touches or crosses the "I am" stroke, forms an oval, and heads to the right. It is important for the last loop formed inside the oval to be wide, without collapsing flat.

The Letter *Q*:

Q q

QUALITY: The letter *Q* speaks of having your work fully express who you are with energy and drive. It is the letter of service to humanity, the "Mother Teresa" letter. Mother Teresa showed a drive and commitment to being of service; this letter can help us develop this quality. This letter also expresses our ability to reach out to others. Whereas the *f* expresses bringing our creativity into the world, the *q* expresses bringing our self into the world.

SUPPORTING SOUL DEVELOPMENT: Service is a very important element in the education at Waldorf schools. There may be children who have difficulty in lovingly and freely being of service; *Q* is the letter for them. Many children will go along with the activity, but only because they have to. *Q* can adjust that attitude into a passion to be of service. For those children who have a hard time reaching out to others to form relationships, whether from pride or fear, this is also the letter (both uppercase and lowercase) to practice.

FORMATION OF THE LETTER: The uppercase *Q* starts with an oval drawn in a clockwise direction that fills the upper and middle zones. The second stroke begins inside the oval and ends outside the oval in the lower zone. This stroke is like a little curvy tail, ending with an upstroke.

The lowercase *q* begins with an oval, then heads vertically into the lower zone, loops up to the left crossing over the vertical line. Here it makes a tie stroke and ends to the right in an upstroke at the baseline. The tie stroke is just under the first oval, like a little pillow on which to rest its head.

The Letter *R*:

R r

QUALITY: This is the letter of innate creativity, of expressing one's unique way of seeing the world. These shapes encourage us not to hold back in sharing our perspective on the world. From the distinctive shape of a hand-carved wooden spoon to a one-of-a-kind perspective drawing, the quality of unique creativity will come out with practice of this letter.

SUPPORTING SOUL DEVELOPMENT: To stimulate creativity in general or in any particular area of study, this is the letter to polish. For children who seem to lack the confidence in their "own ideas" or cannot think of what to draw or what project to take on, *r* is the letter to take up seriously. For artistic inspiration or just plain old "get up and go" to get a project started, practice the letter *R*.

FORMATION OF THE LETTER: The uppercase *R* is formed by first drawing an "I am" stroke. The second stroke starts at the top of the upper zone, forms a backward c, quickly touching the "I am" stroke about the waistline, then sweeping to the right in a diagonal stroke to the baseline.

The lowercase *r* starts at the baseline, heads up to the waistline where it forms a small loop and heads right back up to the waistline in a point, then drops to the baseline and reaches out to join the next letter.

The Letter *S*:

S s

QUALITY: *S* conveys a quality that says, "I am actively calm and calmly active in all situations. In all areas of my life: work, play, sleep, activity, alone time, group time, diet, and exercise, I can gracefully balance each." Balance does not mean that every day each facet is included in exactly the same proportion. Rather, over a week or month, we find the nourishing relationship of each aspect included in our lives, giving us a sense of centered and balanced living. Steiner puts it this way: "A bringing of calm into what has been agitated."

SUPPORTING SOUL DEVELOPMENT: As adults we are more responsible for balance in our young children than they are, but as children mature and develop their own lives, balance becomes an issue for them. For adolescents, it is a true juggling act to spend time with friends, go to school, and do homework in addition to the requirements of home life and possibly a part-time job. *S* will help them balance all these activities.

For the young child, the need to be with others all the time or the desire only to sit inside the house and read are both imbalances. Well-roundedness can be cultivated by practicing the Vimala form of this letter for any child struggling with one-sidedness. This letter will also help to settle down an overactive child.

FORMATION OF THE LETTER: The uppercase *S* is all curves, starting out with a c shape in the upper zone, then swinging to the right to form another c shape, this one backward. The letter ends with a forward-reaching stroke to join the next letter. It is important to keep the shape within the parallel lines drawn from the widest part of the upper and middle zones. Remember there are no angles in this letter.

The lowercase *s* is formed the same way, starting at the waistline and ending in the middle zone, reaching out to join the next letter.

The Letter T :

Т Т

Our writing tells a great deal about us. An experienced person can, with time and effort, learn to "see" many personality traits expressed in a person's handwriting. When we look at writing, each letter carries its own message, tells its own story. For example, the letter T tells us how a person sees his or her role in life. A lowercase t with the t-bar crossed low on the stem (t) can indicate a person has little ambition and an underdeveloped sense of purpose, while a lowercase t with the cross bar at the top shows a person willing to do what is necessary to reach his goals. Assuming this is true, why would we ever teach our children to cross their t three-quarters of the way up the stem, showing only partial enthusiasm for fulfilling their role in life? Don't we want them to have the high self-esteem and strong will power to pursue their dreams with vigor? The Vimala Alphabet shows the t crossed at the top for both the lowercase and uppercase letters. Although this is not familiar to us, it is extremely important. By the way, Rudolf Steiner often crossed his ts at the top, as did many other visionaries.

Crossing the t at the top is one of the hardest handwriting changes for people to get used to visually; I remember my first reaction, "That is strange looking." Yes, at first, it is strange looking. Think about what this says about our culture, that it is strange for people to stand tall and work to achieve their role or purpose in life, giving it their all.

QUALITY: The letter T expresses how I feel about my role in the world and how far I am willing to reach to fulfill it. With the t cross bar crossed at the top for both the lowercase and uppercase letters, it states, "I am willing to reach and stretch tall to find my work and fearlessly do it in the world." It shows willpower, focus, determination, vision and willingness to be visible in the world. Powerful stuff!

SUPPORTING SOUL DEVELOPMENT: Rudolf Steiner says, "T is the streaming of forces from above downward." This letter encourages all of us to get down to the business of doing our work in the world, what we came here to do. Every one of us has a specific role to play in the "theater of life," and each is indispensable and perfect for his or her role. This letter supports all of us, young and old alike, to be everything we can be in life. Everyone can receive something from practicing this letter.

FORMATION OF THE LETTER: The uppercase T is formed with two touching strokes: the "I am" stroke from the upper zone to the baseline and a second stroke that starts in the upper zone and slants up into the upper zone and beyond. Have the cross stroke balance evenly on both sides of the "I am" stroke, with an equal amount of the stroke to the right and to the left of the stem.

The lowercase t starts at the baseline, goes up to the top of the upper zone, then retraces the stem (upstroke) back down to the baseline, where it reaches out to the next letter. The second stroke starts to the left of the long stem and is equally distributed on either side of the upright stroke in the upper zone. The crossbar placed on top of the lowercase t stem supports an orientation toward solutions. The traditional lower placement of the crossbar reinforces an orientation toward problems.

The Letter *V*:

V v

QUALITY: This letter shows us how we sort information and thereby make decisions. In its highest form, this letter can help our choices serve not only us, but also the highest good of the world.

SUPPORTING SOUL DEVELOPMENT: Have you ever had very smart students, but somehow when it comes time to make decisions, they don't consider all the information and consequences and end up making poor choices? Helping them form their *V* exactly as described can make a difference.

Have you ever asked children to clean up after candlemaking and then discover that the "liquid" beeswax has been poured down the drain? Some children don't consider information carefully and need to develop better discernment. There are also children who consider all the options and pick the one that serves only themselves over options that could have served everyone. Try working on the letter *V* for both these types.

FORMATION OF THE LETTER: The uppercase letter begins at the top of the upper zone, angles to the baseline, forming a point and returns to the top of the upper zone. The place where this letter touches the baseline needs to be a point; any curve at the bottom of this letter defeats its power.

The lowercase letter is formed exactly like the uppercase letter, except it occupies only the area between the waistline and the baseline. Remember the point at the baseline.

It is best not to connect this letter to the one before it. I like to have my *V*s stand alone, although they can be connected to the letter that follows.

The Letter *W*:

W W w w

QUALITY: The "double *u*" expresses openness to learning and willingness to share what you know. There is the old saying, "You can lead a horse to water, but you can't make it drink." You can teach children, but you can't make them learn if they are not open. The first half of this letter reveals openness to learning; the second half shows willingness to share one's knowledge.

SUPPORTING SOUL DEVELOPMENT: Have you ever had students who are closed to learning, perhaps because they would rather be doing something else or have had a bad experience in another school? Help your students be open to learning and sharing what they know by encouraging them to form the letter *w* with openness to the upper zone.

FORMATION OF THE LETTER: Like the *M* and *N*, there are two forms of the letter *W*. Please choose the form that will best suit your students. The angled version benefits students who need more intellectual stimulation. The curved form of this letter supports those needing to develop their feeling life.

The uppercase *W* (angled) begins in the upper zone, angles down to the baseline, forming a point and returning at an angle to the top of the upper zone. Here it repeats itself, angling down to the baseline, forming a point and returning to the baseline.

The uppercase *W* (curved) begins in the upper zone, curves down to the baseline, where it curves back up to the upper zone, but not to the top of the upper zone. Then, it descends again the baseline and finishes with a curve back up to the middle of the upper zone.

The lowercase angled *w* follows the shape of the uppercase letter, occupying only the middle zone.

The curved lowercase *w* begins at the waistline, curves down to the baseline, then back up to the waistline. Here it drops back down to baseline, comes almost back to the waistline, where it reaches out to join the next letter with a bridge stroke.

The Letter :

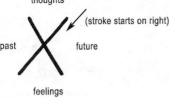

QUALITY: This is the letter of clear confidence in one's abilities, the letter of inner authority. X is a powerful letter that shows how we relate to:

Each of the four sections of the X should be equally formed and open; look for any misshapen sides to uncover issues. For example, I worked with a woman who had traumatically lost her father when she was quite young. She still had unresolved feelings about the past. The area at the bottom of the first stroke (between past and feelings), was oddly shaped, reflecting her unsettled feelings about the past event.

This is one letter that should not ever touch or be connected to another letter. The x always stands alone.

SUPPORTING SOUL DEVELOPMENT: Do you have a child who has a difficult time making decisions? Practicing the X can help strengthen one's inner authority. An X or x that dips down below the baseline can also express the need to punish others for perceived wrongs. Help the child develop a sense of personal power by drawing a Vimala X.

FORMATION OF THE LETTER: The uppercase letter X, starts at the top of the upper zone on the right side with a diagonal stroke to the left ending at the baseline (see diagram for stroke number one). The second, separate stroke for this letter starts at the top of the upper zone on the left (directly above where the first stroke hits the baseline) and heads to the right diagonally to the baseline. It does not touch the next letter.

The lowercase letter is exactly like the uppercase, except it is contained within the middle zone.

Remember this letter stands alone; it is never connected to another letter, before or after it.

The Letter 𝒴 :

𝒴 𝓎

QUALITY: The letter 𝓎 speaks of accepting our gifts and talents with a humble, joyful heart. It gives us an honest assessment of the value of our contribution to others.

Some students excel in one topic, but show less strength in another area. It is healthy for the children to see that we each have our area(s) of talent and places where we experience challenges. Everyone has gifts to share; maybe it's exquisite musical talent or having a grateful heart or a clear mind for math. This is what makes a rich community: the ability to value what each brings to the group, no matter what the gift. We are interrelated through our strengths and weaknesses; we join together in community by sharing our talent and relying on others to share theirs, much as the natural world depends on interrelated ecological systems. The letter 𝓎 represents the first step in this community-building process, helping us accept our own talents as valuable.

SUPPORTING SOUL DEVELOPMENT: Whereas the letter 𝓅 speaks of our feelings of self-lovability, the letter 𝓎 expresses our attitude toward our own accomplishments. Do you have children who don't see the real value of their contributions? Help them practice the letter 𝓎.

FORMATION OF THE LETTER: The uppercase 𝒴 starts at the top of the upper zone with a curving stroke to the baseline that continues to curve back up into the upper zone, forming a cup shape with the right side, slightly lower than the starting stroke. Then it heads down into the lower zone, forming a loop to the left that is about two times the height of the middle zone. The letter ends with the stroke coming gently to the baseline. The cup shape of this letter appears to rest gently on the ending stroke, like a head resting gently on a pillow.

The lowercase letter is formed in the same way, with the cup shape occupying only the middle zone and the lower loop being almost one-and-a-half times the height of the middle zone.

The Letter ꝫ :

ꝫ ꝫ

QUALITY: This is the letter of being at peace with the world and with ourselves. It is said that one sign of enlightenment is ceasing to worry. The letter ꝫ can help us stop worrying and realize the perfection in everything, all unfolding perfectly in its own time. Or, as Steiner says in *Eurythmy as Visible Speech,* there is "a certain lightness in the experience of the z."

SUPPORTING SOUL DEVELOPMENT: Do you have a student who needs to still the mind? Consider those students whose minds seem to race at lightning speed or the poor melancholic who feels sad. Both types can find greater contentment by practicing the Vimala ꝫ.

FORMATION OF THE LETTER: The uppercase letter begins in the upper zone with a curve headed to the right, swinging back in at the waistline. Here it arches out and down into the lower zone, forming a loop about the same height as the midzone, and ending with a stroke coming back up to the baseline.

The lowercase letter ꝫ begins at the waistline with a curve contained in the middle zone, ending at the baseline. Then the stroke goes into the lower zone with a loop to the left about twice the height of the middle zone, ending with the stroke reaching the baseline.

Part Four: Letter Formation Guides

The pages that follow contain examples of forms of the letters to look for and correct in your children's handwriting. The exact meanings of the "undesirable forms" are outside the scope of this book. No single handwriting form stands alone, and when analyzing handwriting one should look for a triad of traits before drawing conclusions about the meaning of the handwriting. The intent of these pages is to educate your eyes to see the forms more clearly and encourage the correct forms in your class's writing.

In general, writing should:

- Slant to the right about five degrees
- Have a uniform slant
- Connect no more than five letters in any word without a break
- Leave a space the size of the lowercase letter *a* between words
- Not touch the lines above or below
- Have one-inch margins on all sides of an 8 ½" x 11" page
- Occupy the appropriate zone(s)
- Have a consistently sized middle zone
- Be on unlined paper turned in landscape direction

For assistance in evaluating the class's handwriting, see the appendix for the "Handwriting Assessment Form."

LETTER: MEANING: UNDESIRABLE FORMS:

A a

Being center stage without ego; stardom

Common Mistakes:

Correction:					
Make oval not round	Too closed, open up oval	Too large, keep within middle zone	Close top (can be chatty)	Keep center open and clear	Slope at 5-degree slant to right

B b

Valuing community; creating win-win situations

Common Mistakes:

Correction:					
Make oval not round	Take out loop in stem	Close bottom of letter	End letter with final stroke to right	Make stem longer	Slope at 5-degree slant to right

LETTER: MEANING: UNDESIRABLE FORMS:

C c

Complete trust

Common Mistakes:

Correction:	Take out loop to start letter	Take out hook to start letter	Too large, keep within middle zone	Too small, fill middle zone	Slope at 5-degree slant to right	Slope at 5-degree slant to right

Đ d

Sensitivity to others; good boundaries

Common Mistakes:

Correction:	Take out loop in stem	Make stem longer	Make stem and oval at same angle	Make oval; fill only middle zone	Use only one stroke	Make oval not round

LETTER: MEANING: UNDESIRABLE FORMS:

E l ε   **Compassion and tolerance**

Common Mistakes:

Correction:	Make full loop	Make narrower loop	Slope at 5-degree slant to right	Too large, keep within middle zone	Take out loop to start letter	Slope at 5-degree slant to right

F f   **Expressing our talents fully**

Common Mistakes:

Correction:	Make three loops	Second loop sweeps to the right	Add tie stroke	No point in lower loop	No point in upper loop	Make three loops

LETTER:	MEANING:	UNDESIRABLE FORMS:

G *g*

Prosperity

Common Mistakes:

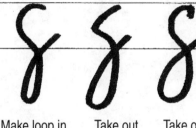

Correction: Use Vimala *g* | Leave midzone open | Make loop in lower zone narrower | Make loop in lower zone wider | Take out angle in midzone | Take out hook

H *h*

Honoring others and expressing it

Common Mistakes:

Correction: Make loop in upper zone taller | Make loop in upper zone | Open space | Make arcade narrower | Make arch shorter | End stroke at baseline

LETTER: MEANING: UNDESIRABLE FORMS:

I i

Clear perception

Common Mistakes:

Correction:	Retrace upstroke	Take out loop in midzone	Use dot, not slash	Place dot directly above stem	Place dot directly above stem	Do not use circle

J j

Intuition

Common Mistakes:

Correction:	Place dot above point	End at baseline	Make dot not dash	Make loop smaller	Make loop wider	Do not use circle

LETTER:	MEANING:	UNDESIRABLE FORMS:

K k

Authority

Common Mistakes:

Correction:	Don't overlap strokes	Take out loops	Take out loops	Keep second stroke all below waistline	End stroke at baseline; do not extend	Slope at 5-degree slant to right

L l

Innate spiritual nature

Common Mistakes:

Correction:	Make wider	Make taller	Take out angles	Start at baseline	End at baseline	Make narrower

LETTER:	MEANING:	UNDESIRABLE FORMS:

Divine grace

Common Mistakes:

Correction:					
Don't retrace downstrokes; have v shape at baseline	First arcade highest, then descending	First arcade highest, then descending	First arcade highest, then descending	Take out angle in intro stroke	Take out loops in downstrokes

Friendship

Common Mistakes:

Correction:					
Take out angle in intro stroke	Don't retrace downstrokes; have v shape at baseline	End at baseline	Take out loops in downstrokes	Needs two arcades	Make first arcade taller than the second

LETTER:	MEANING:	UNDESIRABLE FORMS:

O o

Open communication

Common Mistakes:

Correction:

Take out clutter in oval	Make oval, not round	Make wider	Take out clutter in oval	Too large; keep within middle zone	Make larger

P p

Self-lovability

Common Mistakes:

Correction:

Single "I am" stroke for stem	Take out intro stroke	Press stem against oval	Make oval smaller	Make stem longer	Close oval with loop

LETTER: MEANING: UNDESIRABLE FORMS:

Q q

Service to humanity

Common Mistakes:

Correction:

| Make second stroke smaller | Add tie stroke | Make final loop under oval | Make loops larger | Needs two loops | Rest oval on the stroke |

R r

Innate creativity

Common Mistakes:

Correction:

| Make loop and point | Make loop and point | Use lowercase letter | Make loop smaller | Make even with loop | End stroke at baseline |

LETTER:	MEANING:	UNDESIRABLE FORMS:

S s

Balance

Common Mistakes:

Correction:	Make lower loop wider	Remove curliques	Slope at 5-degree slant to right	Keep within middle zone	Remove all angles	End stroke to the right

T t

My role in the world

Common Mistakes:

Correction:	Place cross stroke at top of stem	Rest cross stroke on stem	Take loop out of stem	Retrace stem	Place crossbar evenly on stem	Place crossbar evenly on stem

LETTER: MEANING: UNDESIRABLE FORMS:

$\mathcal{U}$ u

Receptivity

Common Mistakes:

Correction:	Make less deep	Keep sides straight; leave top open	Remove intro stroke	Make Larger	Keep within middle zone	Retrace upstroke

V v

Discernment

Common Mistakes:

Correction:	Make point at bottom	Omit intro stroke	No loop at base	Make lines straight, not curved	Keep within middle zone	Make less wide

LETTER: MEANING: UNDESIRABLE FORMS:

Open to learning and sharing

Common Mistakes:

Correction:

Make less deep	Open top	Keep sides straight	Make both sides the same	Make wider	Keep within the middle zone

Inner authority

Common Mistakes:

Correction:

Cross in the middle	Take out curves	Form two crossing strokes	Cross in the middle	Form two straight lines	Keep within the middle zone

77

LETTER: MEANING: UNDESIRABLE FORMS:

𝒴 𝓎

Accepting your gifts and talents

Common Mistakes:

Correction:

End stroke at baseline	Add loop in lower zone	Make loop narrower	Omit loop in upper zone	Make loop wider	Make second stroke shorter

𝒵 𝓏

Contentment

Common Mistakes:

Correction:

Don't retrace stroke in middle zone	Make loop smaller	Make loop wider	Eliminate hook	Bring stroke to baseline	Remove loop in the middle zone

Part Five: Practice Pages

This section provides pages for your students to practice writing the letters. Each row starts with an example of the appropriate letter formation. Have your class fill in the rest of the row, practicing the letters slowly and carefully.

Begin by first writing three rows of the letter, both the uppercase and the lowercase. Refer to the beginning letter for the correct form. Next, write at least one row of words that begin with the letter. I have provided a sample word to get started. You can repeat this word, or encourage your students to come up with their own words. Then, practice at least one row of words that contain the letter somewhere within the word. Next, write one line of words that end with the letter being practiced. Fill the rest of the page with free writing (or journaling), paying careful attention to the formation of the letters, especially the ones being practiced.

Remember, you have my permission to reproduce these pages for your students to use as practice pages. (Please do not reproduce other pages in this book; they are copyrighted.)

You can also make your own practice pages for your students using the Vimala alphabet, either from the computer font (available at www.iihs.com) or by very *carefully* handwriting the practice pages. After presenting a letter (uppercase and lowercase), instead of having the children practice only words, you can create sentences using material from your lessons that include the letter being practiced. For example, for the letter G, during a gardening block have your children write: God delights in a growing garden. This will help to enliven your lessons and the children's feel for language while practicing their handwriting.

Name:

Fill in each row:

A a

A a

A a

Angel

bake

area

By permission of the author, this page may be reproduced from *Soul Development through Handwriting* © 2007 Jennifer Crebbin

Name:

Fill in each row:

B b

B b

B b

Boy

able

crab

By permission of the author, this page may be reproduced from *Soul Development through Handwriting* © 2007 Jennifer Crebbin

Name:

Fill in each row:

C c

C c

C c

Courage

achieve

arc

By permission of the author, this page may be reproduced from *Soul Development through Handwriting* © 2007 Jennifer Crebbin

Name:

Fill in each row:

Ð d

Ð d

Ð d

Ðance

middle

child

By permission of the author, this page may be reproduced from *Soul Development through Handwriting* © 2007 Jennifer Crebbin

Name:

Fill in each row:

$\mathcal{E}$ e

$\mathcal{E}$ e

$\mathcal{E}$ e

$\mathcal{E}at$

$after$

$brave$

By permission of the author, this page may be reproduced from *Soul Development through Handwriting* © 2007 Jennifer Crebbin

Name:

Fill in each row:

F f

F f

F f

Fish

effort

relief

By permission of the author, this page may be reproduced from *Soul Development through Handwriting* © 2007 Jennifer Crebbin

Name:

Fill in each row:

G g

G g

G g

Gold

page

being

By permission of the author, this page may be reproduced from *Soul Development through Handwriting* © 2007 Jennifer Crebbin

Name:

Fill in each row:

H h

H h

H h

Help

while

peach

By permission of the author, this page may be reproduced from *Soul Development through Handwriting* © 2007 Jennifer Crebbin

Name:

Fill in each row:

I i

I i

I i

Invite

voice

Hawaii

By permission of the author, this page may be reproduced from *Soul Development through Handwriting* © 2007 Jennifer Crebbin

Name:

Fill in each row:

$\mathcal{J}$ j

$\mathcal{J}$ j

$\mathcal{J}$ j

Juice

adjust

Taj

By permission of the author, this page may be reproduced from *Soul Development through Handwriting* © 2007 Jennifer Crebbin

Name:

Fill in each row:

K k

K k

K k

King

make

work

By permission of the author, this page may be reproduced from *Soul Development through Handwriting* © 2007 Jennifer Crebbin

Name:

Fill in each row:

$\mathcal{L}$ l

$\mathcal{L}$ l

$\mathcal{L}$ l

$\mathcal{L}ight$

$help$

$soil$

By permission of the author, this page may be reproduced from *Soul Development through Handwriting* © 2007 Jennifer Crebbin

Name:

Fill in each row:

M m

M m

M m

Milk

family

from

By permission of the author, this page may be reproduced from *Soul Development through Handwriting* © 2007 Jennifer Crebbin

Name:

Fill in each row:

$\mathcal{N}$ n

$\mathcal{N}$ n

$\mathcal{N}$ n

$\mathcal{Neighbor}$

$candy$

$season$

By permission of the author, this page may be reproduced from *Soul Development through Handwriting* © 2007 Jennifer Crebbin

Name:

Fill in each row:

O o

O o

O o

Open

soon

who

By permission of the author, this page may be reproduced from *Soul Development through Handwriting* © 2007 Jennifer Crebbin

Name:

Fill in each row:

$\mathcal{P}$ p

$\mathcal{P}$ p

$\mathcal{P}$ p

Pretty

aspect

sharp

By permission of the author, this page may be reproduced from *Soul Development through Handwriting* © 2007 Jennifer Crebbin

Name:

Fill in each row:

Q q

Q q

Q q

Quail

acquire

Iraq

By permission of the author, this page may be reproduced from *Soul Development through Handwriting* © 2007 Jennifer Crebbin

Name:

Fill in each row:

R r

R r

R r

Rose

pride

humor

By permission of the author, this page may be reproduced from *Soul Development through Handwriting* © 2007 Jennifer Crebbin

Name:

Fill in each row:

S s

S s

S s

Song

basic

has

By permission of the author, this page may be reproduced from *Soul Development through Handwriting* © 2007 Jennifer Crebbin

Name:

Fill in each row:

T T

T T

T T

Top

pattern

list

By permission of the author, this page may be reproduced from *Soul Development through Handwriting* © 2007 Jennifer Crebbin

Name:

Fill in each row:

𝒰 u

𝒰 u

𝒰 u

Upper

sound

emu

By permission of the author, this page may be reproduced from *Soul Development through Handwriting* © 2007 Jennifer Crebbin

Name:

Fill in each row:

 V v

 V v

V v

Violet

receive

leitmotiv

By permission of the author, this page may be reproduced from *Soul Development through Handwriting* © 2007 Jennifer Crebbin

Name:

Fill in each row:

$\mathcal{W}$ $\mathcal{w}$

$\mathcal{W}$ $\mathcal{w}$

$\mathcal{W}$ $\mathcal{w}$

Wind

Twain

view

By permission of the author, this page may be reproduced from *Soul Development through Handwriting* © 2007 Jennifer Crebbin

Name:

Fill in each row:

X x

X x

X x

X-ray

Text

box

By permission of the author, this page may be reproduced from *Soul Development through Handwriting* © 2007 Jennifer Crebbin

Name:

Fill in each row:

$\mathcal{Y}$ y

$\mathcal{Y}$ y

$\mathcal{Y}$ y

Yellow

system

way

By permission of the author, this page may be reproduced from *Soul Development through Handwriting* © 2007 Jennifer Crebbin

Name:

Fill in each row:

$\mathcal{Z}$ $\mathfrak{z}$

$\mathcal{Z}$ $\mathfrak{z}$

$\mathcal{Z}$ $\mathfrak{z}$

Zebra

size

pizzazz

By permission of the author, this page may be reproduced from *Soul Development through Handwriting* © 2007 Jennifer Crebbin

Appendix

A B C D E F G H I J K L M N O P Q R

a
b
c
d
e
f
g
h
i

S
T
U
V
W
X
Y
Z

Handwriting Assessment of:

<u>Quality:</u>	<u>Assessment:</u>

Slant: Five-degree slope

              Uniformity

Spacing: Within a word

              Between words (size of an "a")

              Between lines

Margins: 1 inch on all sides of 8½ x 11 inch page

Size: Lowercase letters

              Uppercase letters

Shape: Lowercase letters

              Uppercase letters

Comments:

j k l m n o p q r s t u v w x y z

By permission of the author, this page may be reproduced, from *Soul Development through Handwriting* © 2007 Jennifer Crebbin

Five-degree Page Liner

By permission of the author, this page may be reproduced from *Soul Development through Handwriting* © 2007 Jennifer Crebbin

By permission of the author, this page may be reproduced from *Soul Development through Handwriting* © 2007 Jennifer Crebbin

111

Bibliography

Dinklage, Helen, *Therapy through Handwriting,* Mercury Press, Spring Valley, NY, 1981 (1978).

Getty, Barbara, and Inga DuBay, *Instruction Manual,* 2nd ed., Italic Handwriting Series, Continuing Education Publications, Portland, OR, 1979.

Gladich, Joen, and Paula Sassi, *The "Write" Approach: Form Drawing for Better Handwriting,* vols. 1 & 2, Rudolf Steiner College Press, Fair Oaks, CA, 1991.

Glöckler, Michaela and Wolfgang Goebel, *A Guide to Child Health,* 3rd ed., Floris Books, Edinburgh, 2007.

Green Meadow High School Faculty, "In Praise of Cursive Writing," *Renewal,* spring/summer 2005, vol. 14, no. 1.

König, Karl, *On Reading and Writing: Toward a Phenomenology and Pathology of Literacy,* Camphill Books, 2002.

McAllen, Audrey, *Teaching Children Handwriting: Historical, Developmental, and Practical Aspects of Writing,* Rudolf Steiner College Press, 2002.

McAllen, Audrey, and Irene Ellis, "Teachers, Look to your Handwriting," Mary Ellen Willby, ed., *Learning Difficulties: A Guide for Teachers: Waldorf Insights and Practical Approaches,* Rudolf Steiner College Press, Fair Oaks, CA, 1998.

Preston, Michael, "Paper, Pen, and Child: Teaching the Endangered Art of Handwriting," *Renewal,* spring/summer 2003, vol. 12, no. 1.

Bibliography

Rodgers, Vimala, *Change Your Handwriting, Change Your Life*, Celestial Arts, Berkeley, CA, 1993.

———*Your Handwriting Can Change Your Life*, Simon and Schuster, New York, 2000.

———*The Vimala System: Character Building through Simplified Handwriting*, IIHS, Nevada City, 2006.

Steiner, Rudolf, *The Alphabet: An Expression of the Mystery of Man*, Mercury Press, Spring Valley, NY, 1982 (lecture, December 18, 1921).

———*Art in the Light of Mystery Wisdom*, Rudolf Steiner Press, London, 1970.

———*Balance in Teaching*, SteinerBooks, Great Barrington, MA, 2007.

———*Eurythmy as Visible Speech*, Anastasi, (U.K.), 2005 (June 24–July 12, 1924).

———*Isis Mary Sophia, Her Mission and Ours*, SteinerBooks, Great Barrington, MA, 2003.

———*Practical Advice to Teachers*, Anthroposophic Press, Great Barrington, MA, 2000.

———*Rosicrucianism and Modern Initiation*, lecture 6, Jan. 13, 1924, Rudolf Steiner Press, London, 1965.

———*The Foundations of Human Experience*, Anthroposophic Press, Great Barrington, MA, 1996.

———*The Spiritual Ground of Education*, Anthroposophic Press, Great Barrington, MA, 2004.

Working Material for the Class Teacher: Forming the Lessons of Grades One through Eight, 1994, Study Material of the Pedagogical Section and the Pedagogical Research Center.

Resources for Making and Writing with Goose Feather Quill Pens

http://www.geocities.com/Athens/Delphi/7958/quill-page-color.htm
http://medievalwriting.50megs.com/tools/quill.htm Dr. Dianne Tillotson
http://www.jasa.net.au/quillpen.htm

For your convenience, the Vimala Alphabet is available both as a computer font and pre-printed on 8½ x 11 inch, bright yellow card stock. You can order these and other items, by visiting Vimala Rodgers' webpage at www.iihs.com or by completing the order form below:

Institute of Integral Handwriting Studies
Post Office Box 804
Nevada City, CA 95959-0804
E-mail: teachers@iihs.com

Within the USA we ship all orders Priority Mail. For all other orders we ship First Class International. Please inquire about shipping and handling costs if ordering from outside the USA.

Quantity	Product	Amount
	Vimala Alphabet Font compatible with Windows or Mac	$49.95
	The Vimala Alphabet – 32 cards for the classroom bright yellow 8 ½ x 11 inch cards	24.00
		Subtotal:
	California residents: add 7 ½ % sales tax (subtotal x .075)	**CA tax:**
	Shipping / handling: $5.50 (1st item); $2.10 (each additional item)	**Shipping:**
		ORDER TOTAL: